WHAT MATTERS MOST?

ENERGY and POWER

Paul Mason
Nigel Baines

Gareth Stevens
PUBLISHING

Please visit our website, www.garethstevens.com. For a free color catalog of all our high-quality books, call toll free 1-800-542-2595 or fax 1-877-542-2596.

Cataloging-in-Publication Data

Names: Mason, Paul, author. | Baines, Nigel, illustrator.
Title: Energy and power / by Paul Mason, illustrated by Nigel Baines.
Description: Buffalo, NY : Gareth Stevens Publishing, 2026. |
Series: What matters most? | Includes glossary and index.
Identifiers: ISBN 9781482475579 (pbk.) | ISBN 9781482475586 (library bound) |
ISBN 9781482475593 (ebook)
Subjects: LCSH: Force and energy--Juvenile literature.
Classification: LCC QC73.M37 2026 | DDC 531.113--dc23

Published in 2026 by
Gareth Stevens Publishing
2544 Clinton St.
Buffalo, NY 14224

First published in Great Britain in 2024 by Wayland

Editor: Sarah Peutrill
Illustrator: Nigel Baines

Printed in China
CPSIA compliance information: Batch #QW26GS: For further information contact Gareth Stevens at 1-800-542-2595.

Contents

Which energy matters most?

WHIRR!
SPIN!
CRACKLE!
Welcome to the world of energy and power. MY world. I'm Tina Turbine. Turbines like me make electricity for you.
Think of all the things you need electricity for. Without electricity you couldn't charge your phone ...

Argh! Now what do I do?

Electricity chases away the dark ...

In fact, electricity is used for all kinds of things ...

To make electricity, turbines like me need energy from other places. As we receive the energy, we spin faster and faster, and turn the spinning into electricity.

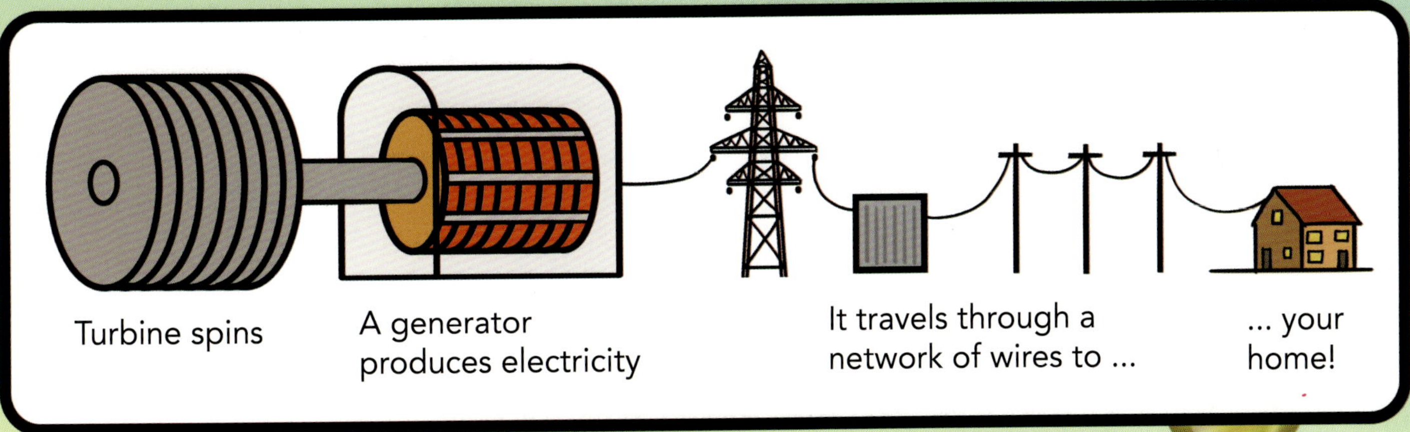
Turbine spins
A generator produces electricity
It travels through a network of wires to ...
... your home!

Electricity, and the energy to heat homes and power vehicles, can come from LOTS of sources. But which one matters most?

Definitely me.

I'm sure it's me – the powerful wind!
Me.
I'm shiny and new. It must be me?

The sun

Heat and light

Look, no one likes a show-off ... so I'll just say that I heat the WHOLE WORLD every day.
You must have noticed that I keep people warm and help them to see – part of each day, anyway.

My energy also lets plants grow. Animals and people can eat the plants. And humans also burn plants, such as wood, for heat and light.

Fossil fuels are the remains of plants or animals that used my energy to grow millions of years ago.

Coal

Gas

Oil

Heat and light goes from the sun to Earth

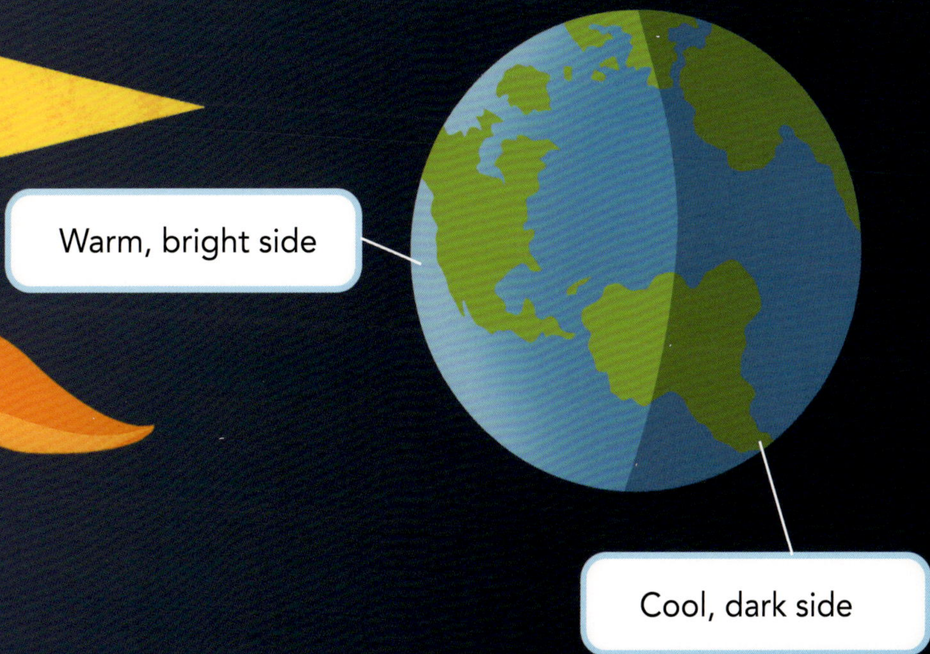

So, I heat the world, feed the world, and fuel the world. I think it's pretty clear which kind of energy matters most – don't you?

Coal

Burning power

The sun is always trying to be the center of attention.

To be honest, if you use electricity at all, you should probably thank ME for all my sacrifices. Let me explain ...

❶ I'm dug out

I'm a rock that has to be dug out of the ground. Sometimes I'm buried as much as a 0.6 mile (1 km) underground.

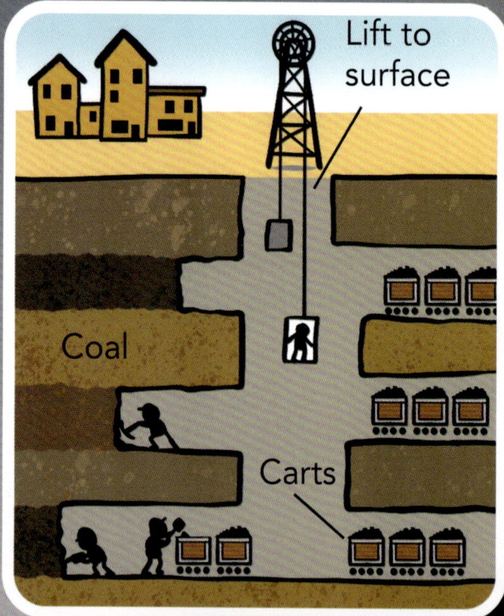

2 Next I'm crushed

I did tell you
I make sacrifices!

3 Then I'm burned

This heats water, which makes steam to turn a turbine.

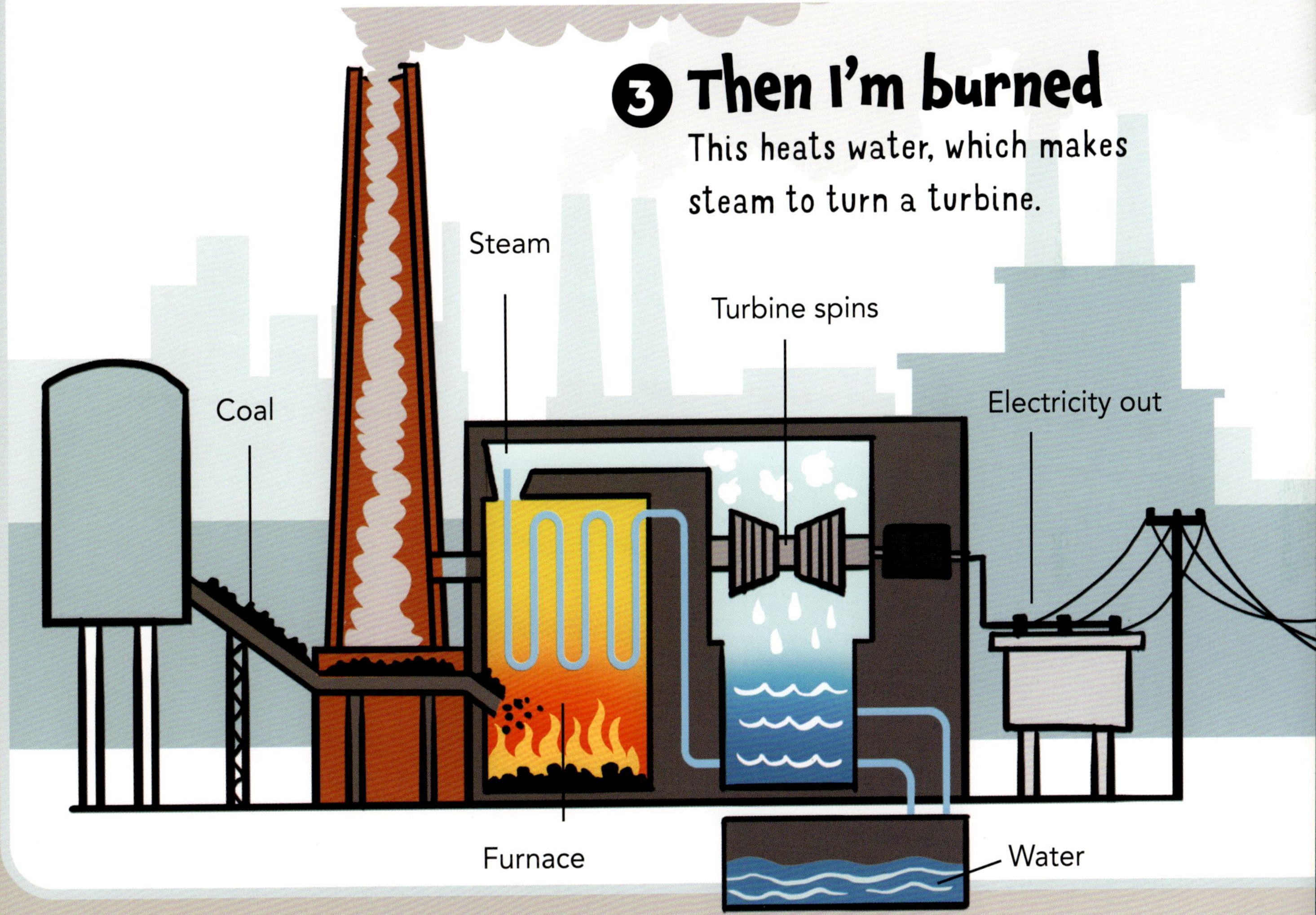

About a third of all the world's electricity is made by burning me – which means I matter a LOT.

Natural gas

Energy from flames

I'd been resting underground for MILLIONS of years – then someone sucked me up to the surface!

I didn't mind, actually: it was getting a bit boring down there. Next, I whooshed along pipelines that took me all over the place.

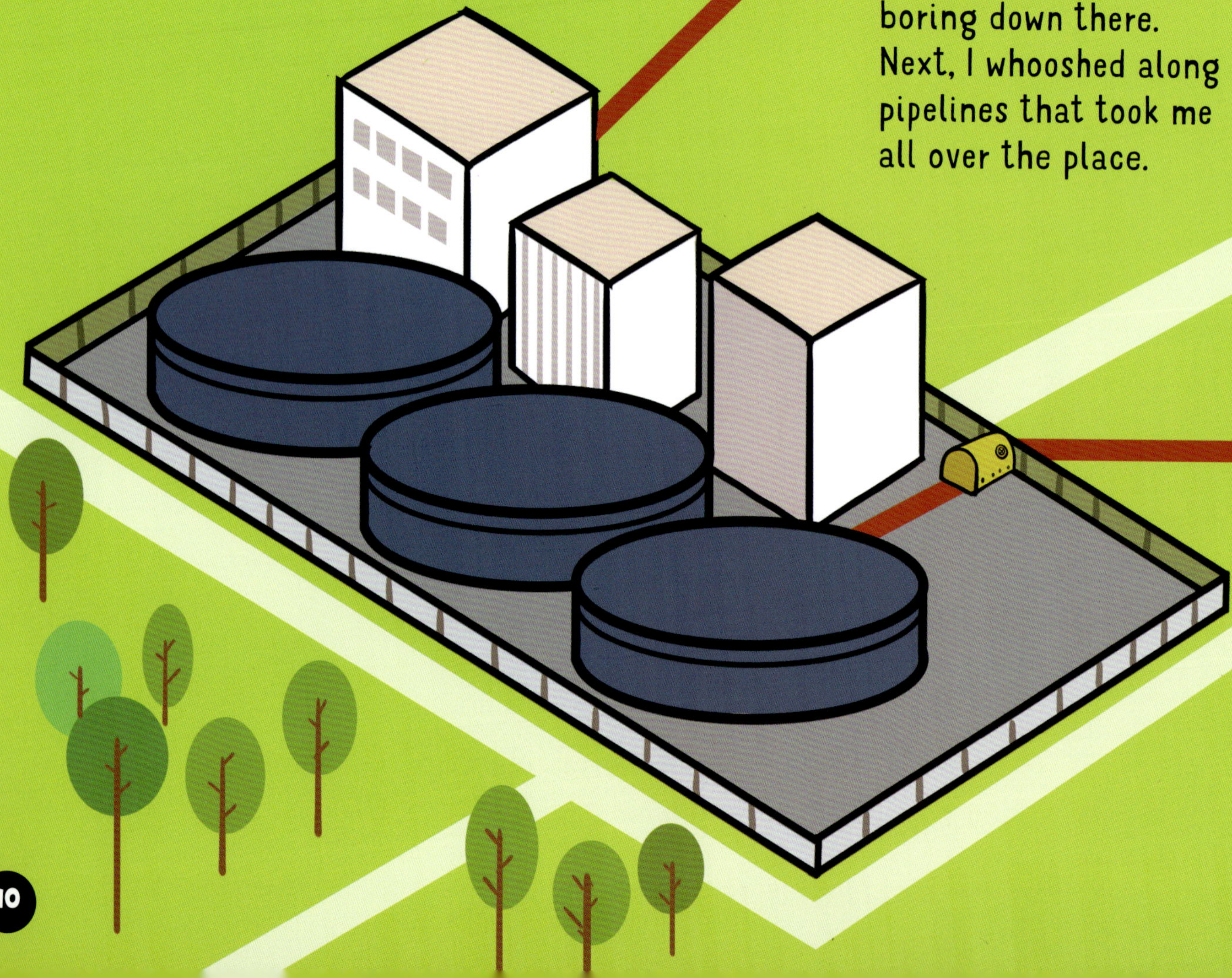

I went to a power station's turbine room – where they set me alight.

I visited people's houses. They set me alight there too.

I get pumped into boilers to heat up water.

I even got turned into fertilizer to help crops grow. Instead of setting me alight, they buried me.

It's all very exciting – I just wish people didn't keep burning me as soon as I arrive! Anyway, all those jobs are important to a LOT of people, so surely I matter?

Oil

Transport power

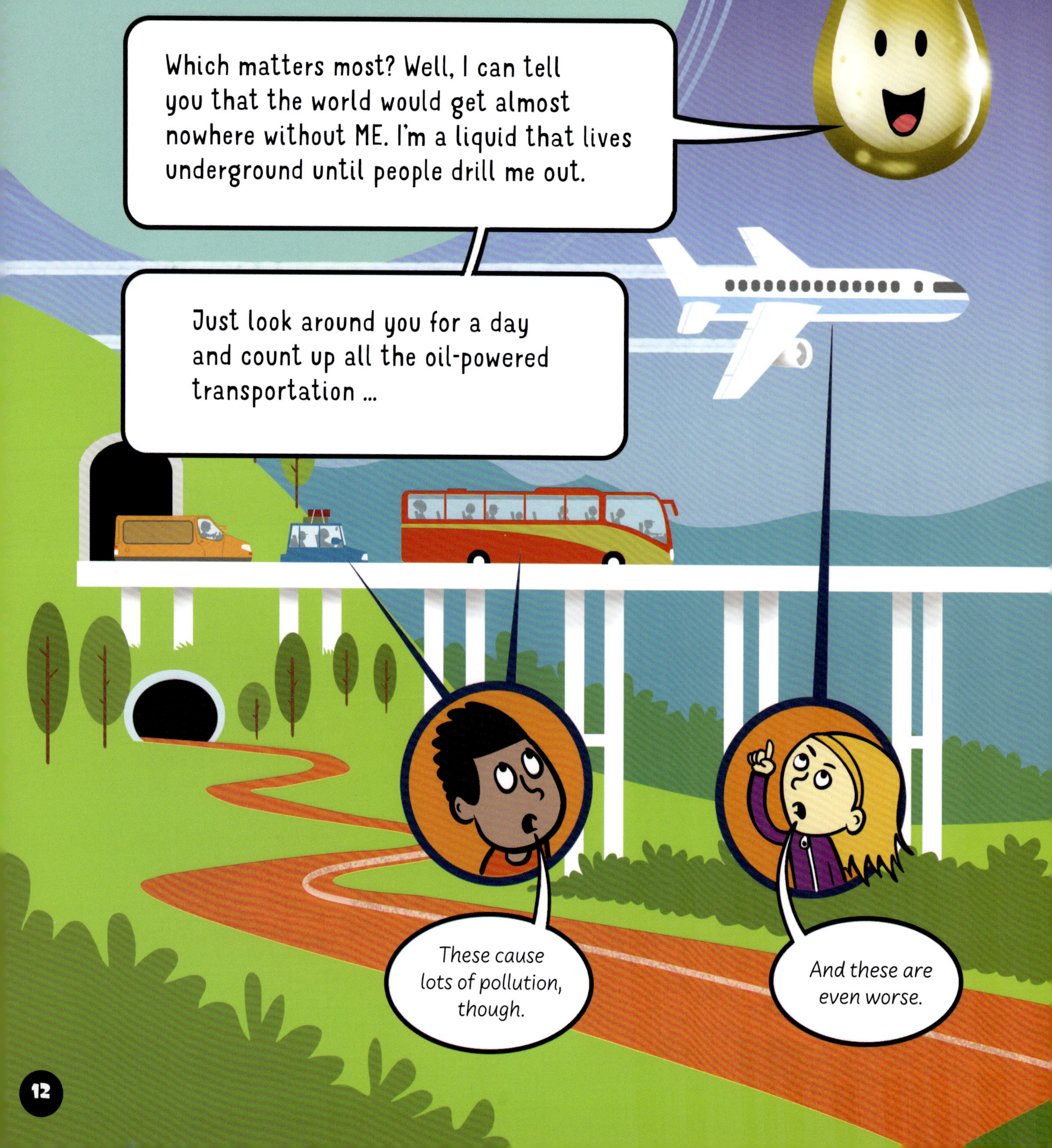

Which matters most? Well, I can tell you that the world would get almost nowhere without ME. I'm a liquid that lives underground until people drill me out.
Just look around you for a day and count up all the oil-powered transportation ...
These cause lots of pollution, though.
And these are even worse.

As well as for transportation, exploding oil is also used to heat buildings and produce electricity.

(And did you know that most plastics are made using oil?)

Imagine what would happen without me. No one could travel at all!. Unless they wanted to walk ... or skateboard ... or scooter ... or bike.

This is much nicer.
Cheap too.
Lovely fresh air.
And healthy.
OK, maybe you COULD get around without me. I still matter, though! Don't I?

Global warming

Yes, fossil fuels such as coal, gas, and oil are everywhere – in fact, the modern world was built using them.
The trouble is, fossil fuels come with a MASSIVE problem ...

❶ Chemicals are released

When we process and use fossil fuels, chemicals are released as gases.

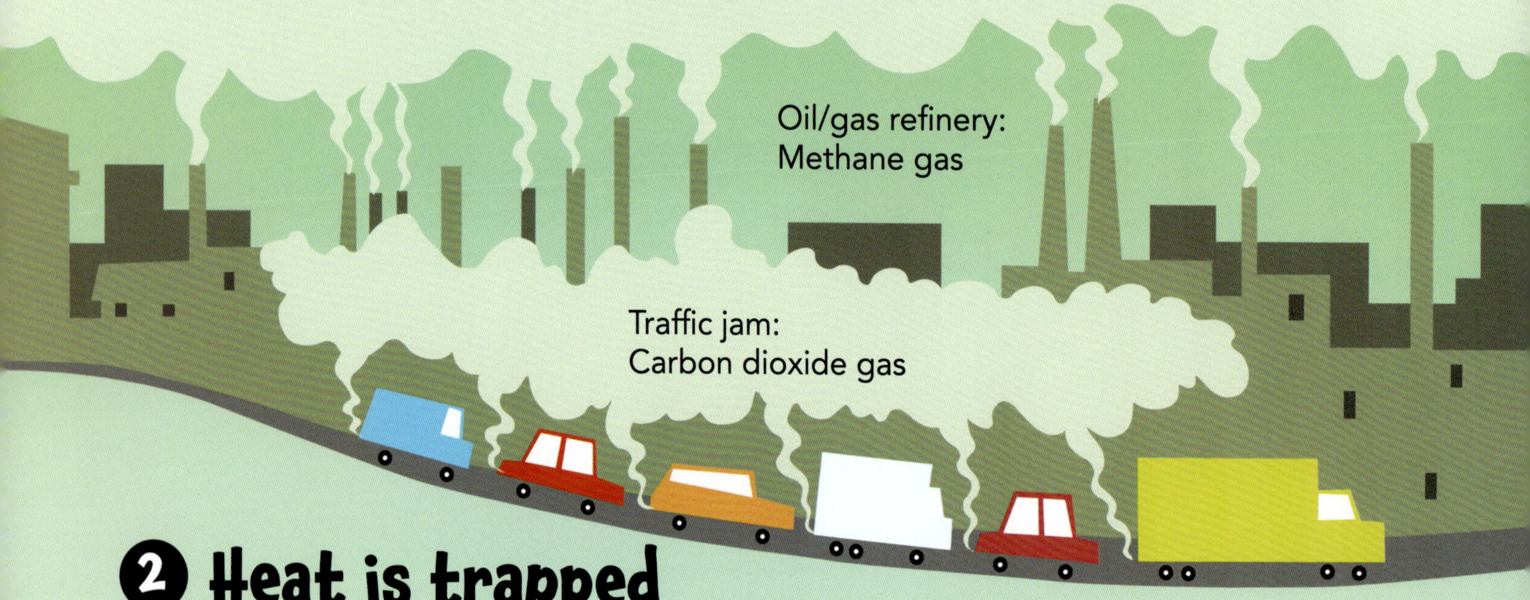
Oil/gas refinery:
Methane gas
Traffic jam:
Carbon dioxide gas

❷ Heat is trapped

These gases rise into the atmosphere. Here they trap heat, like the glass in a greenhouse.

3 Earth's temperature rises

The trapped heat is slowly raising Earth's average temperature and causing many problems:

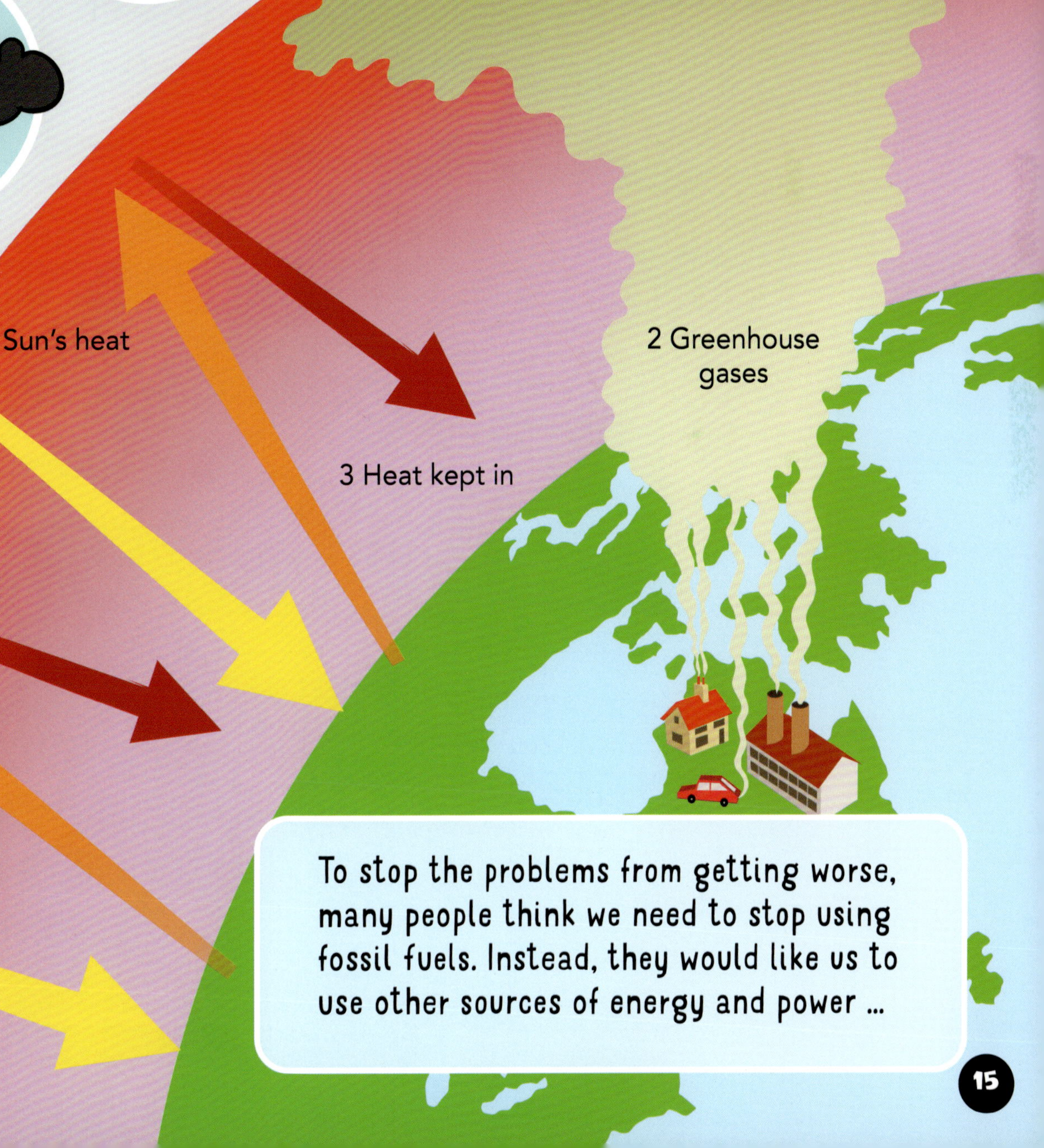

To stop the problems from getting worse, many people think we need to stop using fossil fuels. Instead, they would like us to use other sources of energy and power ...

Solar

Electrifying sunshine

Honestly, digging up fossil fuels and setting light to them? What a fuss! Solar panels like me make electricity just from sunshine.

It was in the 1950s when the first solar panels started to be used.

During the 1950s, we solar panels helped humans explore space – and we're still there today.

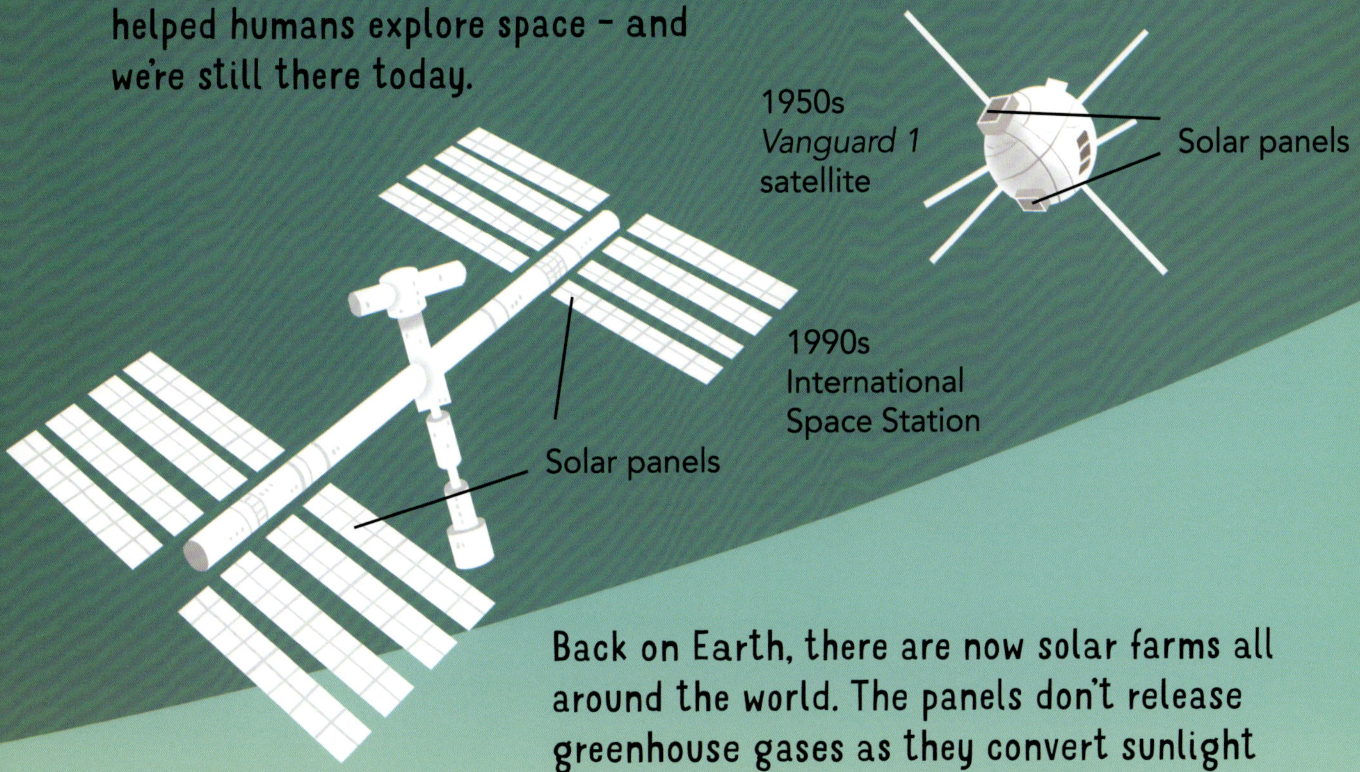

Back on Earth, there are now solar farms all around the world. The panels don't release greenhouse gases as they convert sunlight into electricity.

Each year, more of your electricity comes from solar panels like me. I matter now, but I'll matter even more in the future.

Wind

Spinning energy

Whoosh! Woo-hoo! Yes, of COURSE you can use a bit of my energy as I whizz past.
My energy is actually REALLY useful for pushing things! I can push the sails of a ship or a windsurfer.
I can also push the blades of a propellor or a windmill to make them spin.
I actually make the waves too.

I'm spinning around, move out of my wa-ay ...
Will you STOP singing that?
You know what you can use a turning movement for, don't you? YES! Making electricity!
So, I'm freely available, I don't release any gases, I won't ever stop blowing, and I don't take up lots of space (unlike a solar farm). What could be better than me?

Water

Rivers and dams

Honestly, Wind is SUCH an old windbag. I'm just as good at spinning turbines, but I make less noise about it.

All you need is water and gravity.* Gravity is the force that pulls water downhill.

1 Water is stored

A large store of water, or reservoir, builds up behind a dam.

*And a hydroelectric power station

2 Water flows down

It goes along passages.

3 Turbine turns

The water flows through a turbine. This produces electricity.

Dams may stop fish from swimming upstream. Fish ladders give them a way to get up the river.

This is hard work.
Why can't we have an escalator?

4 Electricity flows

It is carried to wherever it is needed.

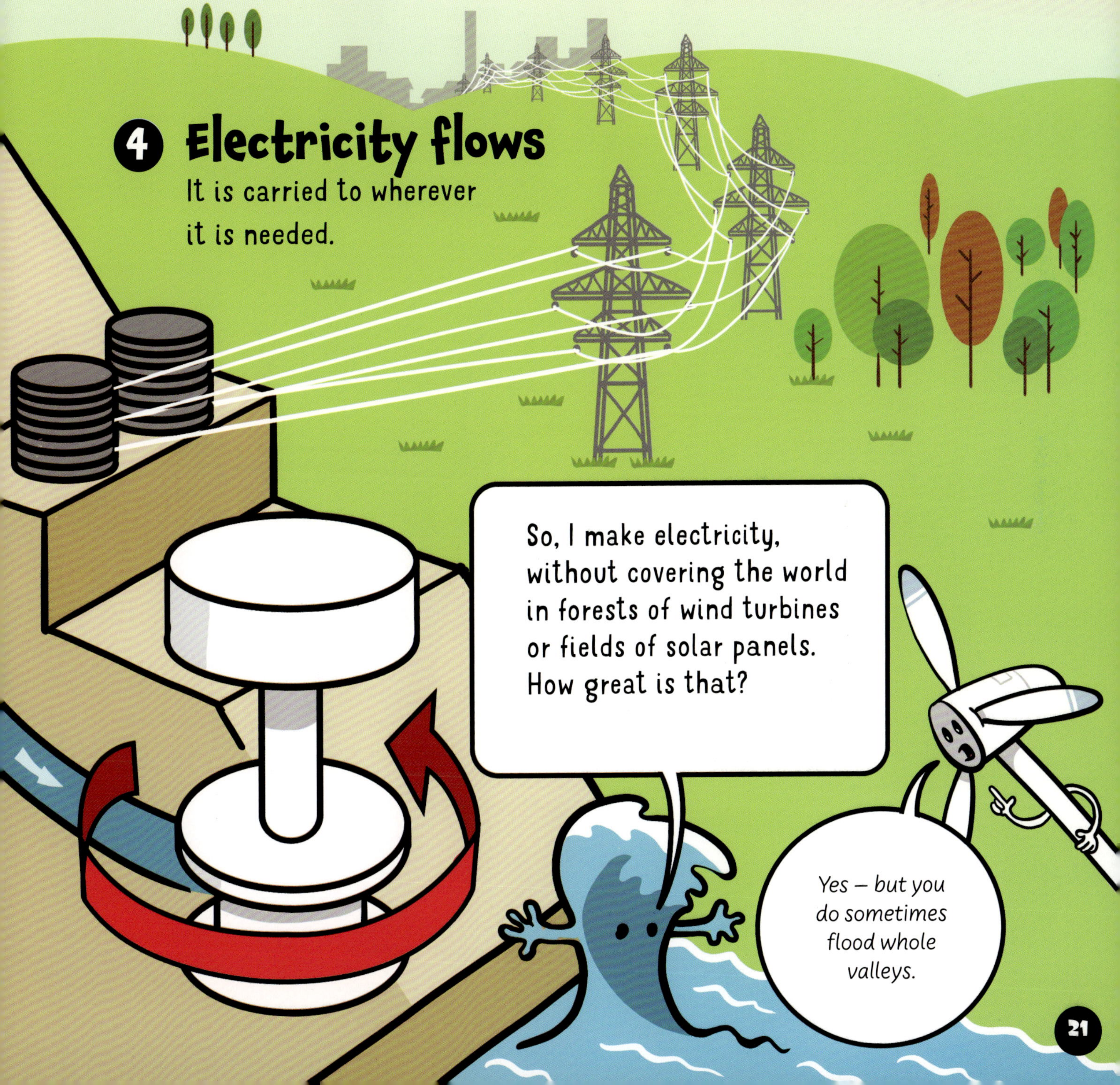
So, I make electricity, without covering the world in forests of wind turbines or fields of solar panels. How great is that?
Yes – but you do sometimes flood whole valleys.

Tidal

Energy from the ocean

I'm pretty sure I'm the mightiest. After all, you humans can't yet harness the power of my waves.
Tidal currents rotate turbine blades

But humans DO use the neverending flow of my tides to get energy and power.

Already I'm helping to provide electricity around the world – and the electricity can be used thousands of miles from the ocean.

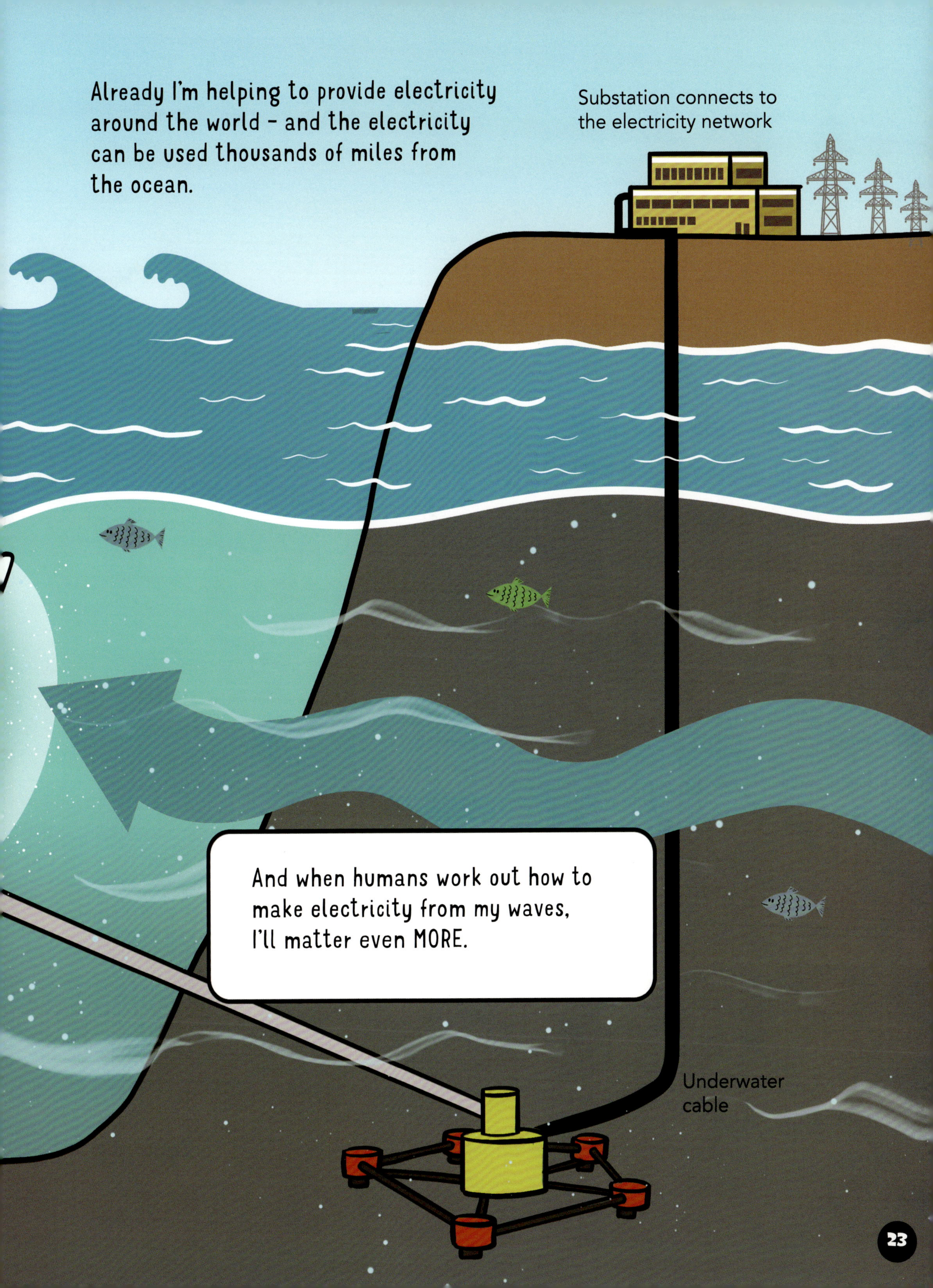

And when humans work out how to make electricity from my waves, I'll matter even MORE.

Earth

Underground energy

I can tell you a MUCH easier place to get energy than a big whoosh of water. Under your feet!

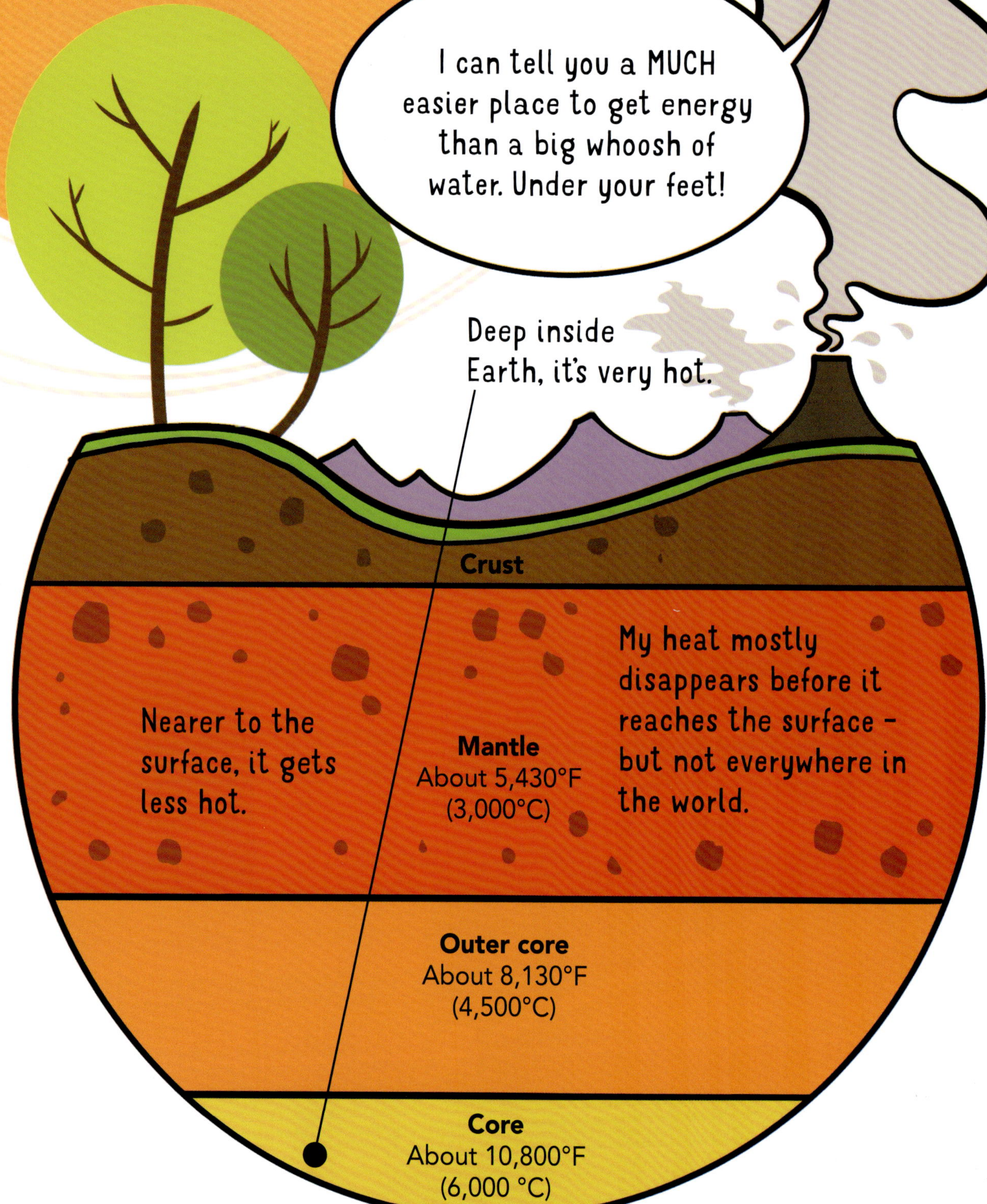
Deep inside Earth, it's very hot.
Crust
Nearer to the surface, it gets less hot.
Mantle
About 5,430°F (3,000°C)
My heat mostly disappears before it reaches the surface – but not everywhere in the world.
Outer core
About 8,130°F (4,500°C)
Core
About 10,800°F (6,000 °C)

In some places, there's enough heat to power turbines and make electricity. It works like this:

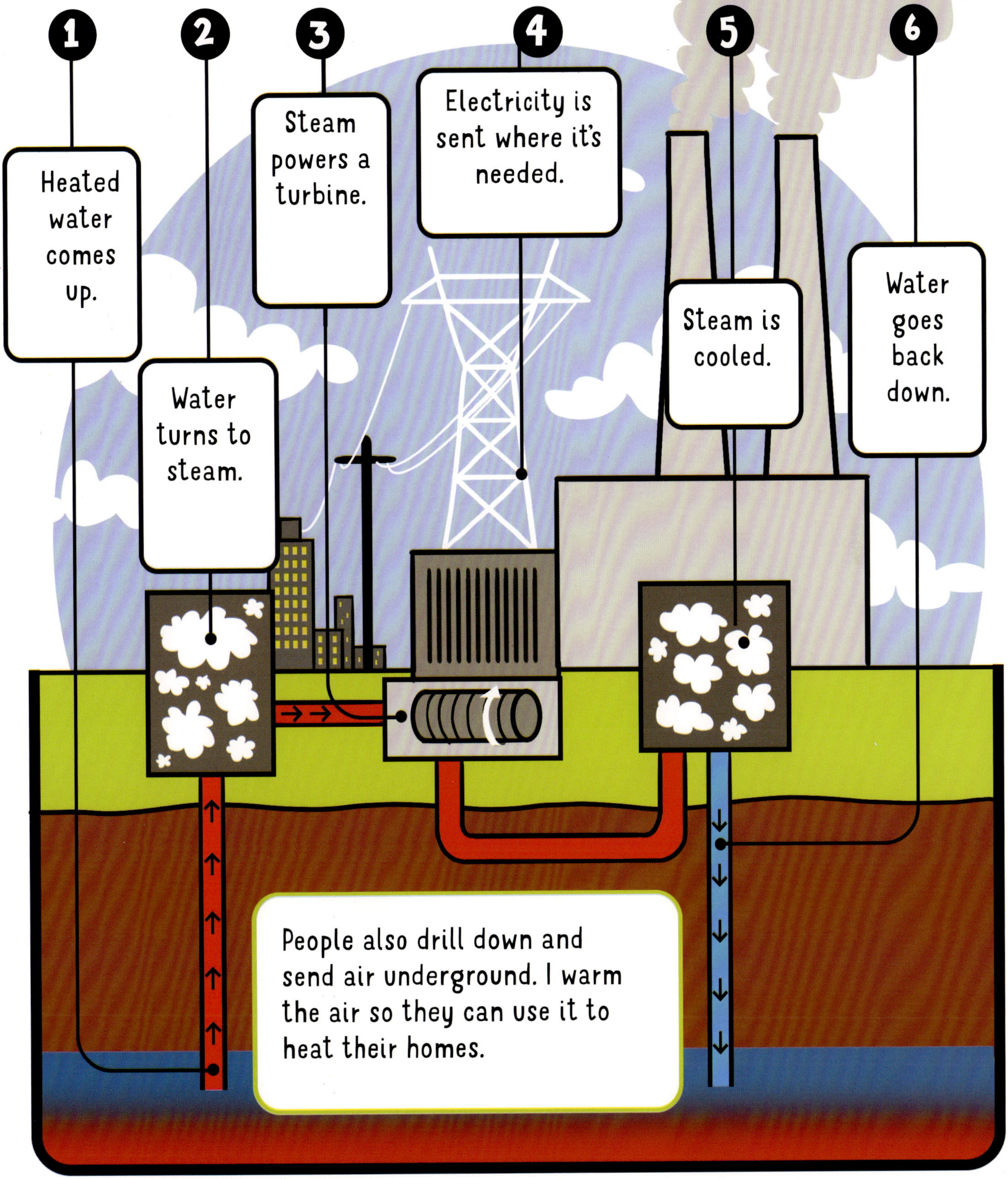
1
Heated water comes up.
2
Water turns to steam.
3
Steam powers a turbine.
4
Electricity is sent where it's needed.
5
Steam is cooled.
6
Water goes back down.

People also drill down and send air underground. I warm the air so they can use it to heat their homes.

What could be better than using the planet's underground heat to give everyone energy?

Nuclear

Atomic energy

Well, yes, since you ask ... I AM stylish and modern. Coal and friends are really stuffy and old.

I get my energy from splitting tiny little atoms.

Nuclear fission

WOO-HOO!
Watch out!

1 Neutron: fired at the heart of a uranium atom

2 The atom splits

Nuclear fission releases a lot of energy. This is used to make steam. The steam spins a turbine, which produces electricity.

4 The released energy heats water and makes steam

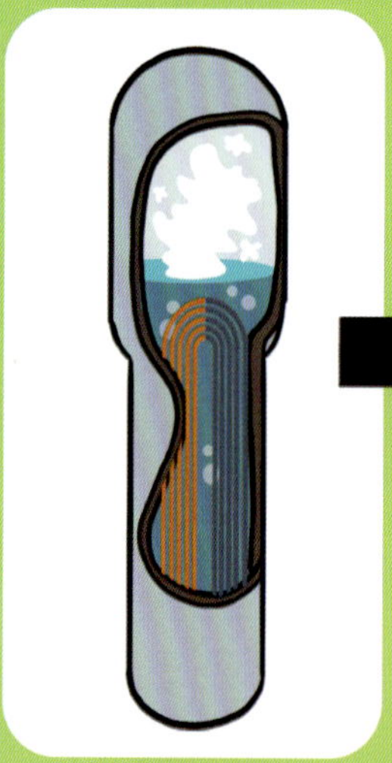

5 The steam spins turbines

Atoms are too small even to see, but splitting one releases a LOT of heat.

I brought my hammer. Let's start splitting atoms!
Is this your first day in the lab?

BOOM!
AAH!
OW!

3 Energy is released and more neutrons fire off. These hit more atoms and a chain reaction starts

There is one small problem – the waste I make kills living things, and poisons the earth, water, and air. It has to be kept VERY safe.

6 Electricity is sent where it is needed

If something goes wrong, I might matter more than all the others – just not in a good way.

And the winner is ...

So, which energy matters most?
The sun wins. It keeps us warm and provides light – without anyone having to do anything at all.
Told you so.

Fossil fuels do so much harm to the planet that they can't win.

The other energies do less harm. They come somewhere in between.

Second place isn't bad.
I think I came second, though?
No, me!

Glossary

atom a tiny building block. All things are made of atoms.

chemical a material that changes other materials when they are mixed.

coal a brown or black rock usually found underground, which can be dug up and burned to produce energy. Coal is a type of fossil fuel.

fossil fuels sources of energy, such as coal, gas, and oil, that were formed in the ground from dead plants and animals over millions of years

greenhouse gases gases that surround Earth and act like a blanket to keep in heat

hydroelectric using flowing water to make electricity

natural gas a gas that is found naturally underground. It can be removed and burned to produce energy. Natural gas is a type of fossil fuel.

neutron a tiny part of an atom

oil a liquid that is buried underground, and can be removed and burned to produce energy. Oil is a type of fossil fuel.

refinery a place where materials are turned into useful products.

steam water that has become a gas after being heated

tide the regular change in how far up or down the land the ocean reaches

turbine a machine that spins very fast to produce electricity

uranium a chemical substance that is used as a fuel in nuclear power plants

Energy usage

Around the world, we still get most of our energy from fossil fuels. Each year, though, a little more comes from other sources.

Sources of world electricity

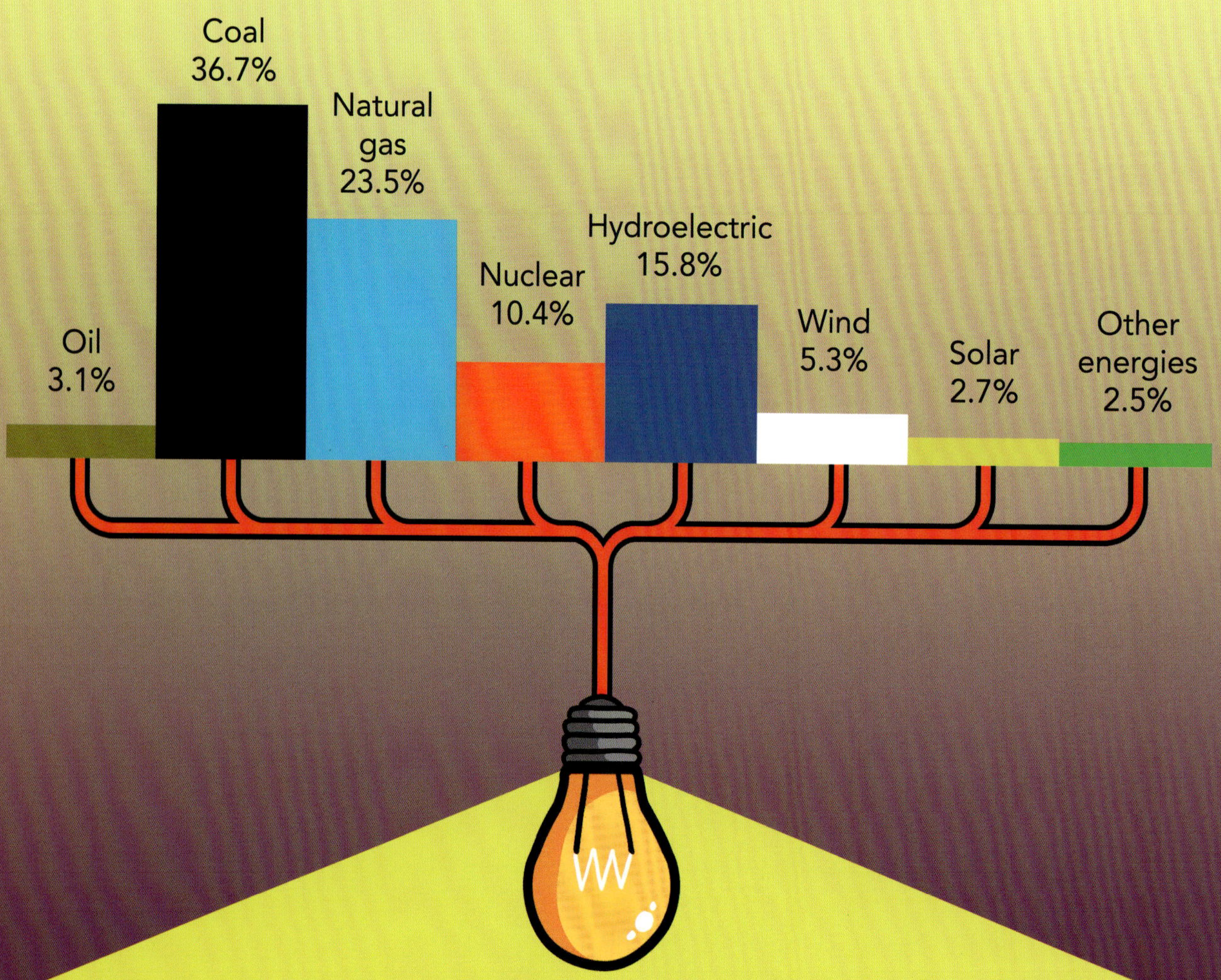

In 2019, nearly two-thirds of the world's electricity was made by burning fossil fuels. Over one-third of world electricity came from coal.

Maybe I should stay underground.
Sorry.

Coal is our dirtiest energy source and makes the most greenhouse gases. Oil and gas are also very polluting.

The non-fossil fuels – nuclear, wind, and solar – produce the least pollution. The good news is that they make more of our electricity each year. Solar and wind power are the fastest growing.

We TOLD you so!

Index